PREDATORS OF

North America

Michael Tylers

Cavendish Square

New York

Published in 2015 by Cavendish Square Publishing, LLC
243 5th Avenue, Suite 136, New York, NY 10016

First Edition

Website: cavendishsq.com

This publication represents the opinions and views of the author based on his or her personal experience, knowledge, and research. The information in this book serves as a general guide only. The author and publisher have used their best efforts in preparing this book and disclaim liability rising directly or indirectly from the use and application of this book.

CPSIA Compliance Information: Batch #WW15CSQ

All websites were available and accurate when this book was sent to press.

Library of Congress Cataloging-in-Publication Data

Tylers, Michael, 1959- author.
Predators of North America / Michael Tylers.
pages cm. — (World's scariest predators)
Includes bibliographical references and index.
ISBN 978-1-50260-185-8 (hardcover) ISBN 978-1-50260-184-1 (paperback) ISBN 978-1-50260-183-4 (ebook)
1. Predatory animals—North America—Juvenile literature. 2. Predation (Biology)—Juvenile literature. I. Title.

QL758.T95 2015
591.53—dc23

2014024984

Editor: Kristen Susienka
Senior Copy Editor: Wendy A. Reynolds
Art Director: Jeffrey Talbot
Designer: Douglas Brooks
Senior Production Manager: Jennifer Ryder-Talbot
Production Editor: David McNamara
Photo Researcher: J8 Media

The photographs in this book are used by permission and through the courtesy of:
Corbis: 17 (Royalty Free), 20 (Royalty Free)
Dreamstime: 8 (Jumoku), 8 (Valentina 75), 12 (Surz 01), 13 (Bernhard Richter), 20 (Outdoorsman),
24 (Erik Manore), 25 (Moose Henderson), 28 (Steve Byland), 29 (Brian Lasnby)
FLPA: 17 (Paul Sawer), 21 (Paul Sawer), 28 (Albert Lleal)
Photos.com: 9, 16, 24
U.S. Fish & Wildlife Services: 12.

Printed in the United States of America

Contents

Did You Know?
North America is the
third-largest continent
on Earth.

Introduction

The world is full of many animals. Each animal is different, with its own characteristics. Some animals have lots of fur and four legs, while others have silky scales and travel around on their bellies. Sometimes, one of the characteristics that make them different is that they are frightening.

North America has many animals, such as birds, wild cats, wolves, and snakes. Some of these animals are harmless. Others are very big and have large claws and teeth. Some of the scariest animals are not large, but they have a poisonous bite or sting.

This book will tell you many fascinating facts about some of the scariest and most interesting animals in North America. Remember that many of these animals may live near you, so if you see one, keep a safe distance.

Barn Owl

Scientific Name: *Tyto alba*

The barn owl is an animal that hunts other, smaller animals. Every inch of this creature is designed to make it the perfect hunter. Its long wings are made for slow flight, allowing the owl to take its time locating its prey. Soft feathers on the edge of each wing mean that it can fly silently. While the barn owl has excellent eyesight, it can hunt in total darkness, too, thanks to its super-sensitive hearing. In fact, its curious heart-shaped face works like a sonar dish, directing sound toward the owl's ears. Barn owls mainly hunt **nocturnal** animals such as mice, shrews, and voles.

= Habitat

Where in the World?

It is believed that there are around thirty-five **subspecies** of barn owls. These adaptable birds are found all over the world, although they avoid desert and Arctic regions. They like open countryside, near farms or woods.

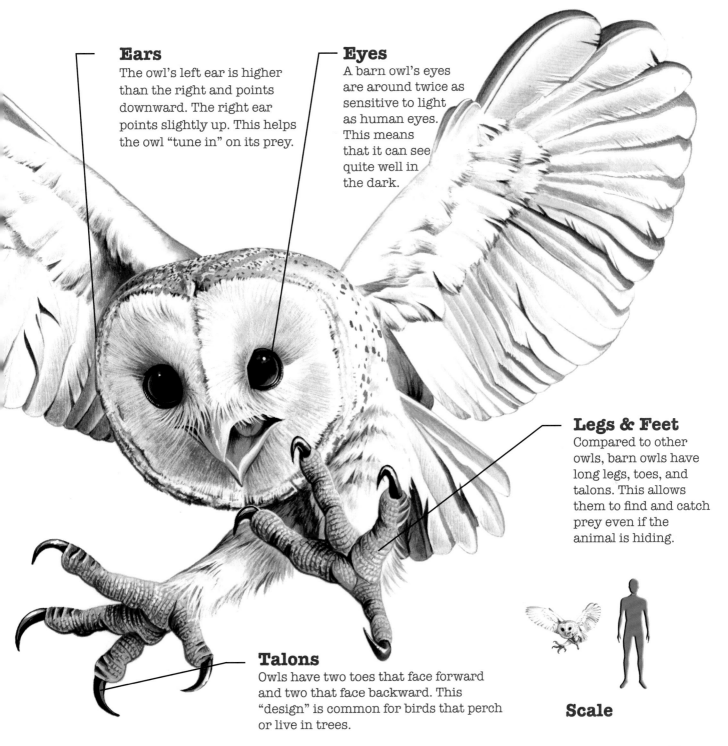

Ears
The owl's left ear is higher than the right and points downward. The right ear points slightly up. This helps the owl "tune in" on its prey.

Eyes
A barn owl's eyes are around twice as sensitive to light as human eyes. This means that it can see quite well in the dark.

Legs & Feet
Compared to other owls, barn owls have long legs, toes, and talons. This allows them to find and catch prey even if the animal is hiding.

Talons
Owls have two toes that face forward and two that face backward. This "design" is common for birds that perch or live in trees.

Scale

The barn owl's heart-shaped face helps direct sound toward its ears.

Ferocious Fact

Barn owls are nocturnal but can also be seen hunting during the day, usually over open fields. Sometimes they are spotted flying slowly back and forth in search of prey. This is called quartering, a technique used to carefully locate their victims. For nighttime flight, the barn owl's wings have feathers that absorb sound and make their flying silent.

A barn owl swoops down on its prey.

Did You Know?

- Owls swallow their food whole. Any parts that can't be digested are later regurgitated, or coughed up, in the form of a **pellet**.

- On average, a barn owl catches and eats four small mammals every night. That's 1,460 animals each year!

- Together a male and female barn owl usually have two broods, or families, a year. Each brood can include up to eleven eggs.

Owls are fearsome predators, capable of taking down a number of prey in one night.

Polar Bear

Scientific Name: *Ursus maritimus*

The polar bear is the world's largest land-based **carnivore**. This creature spends its life in the Arctic where temperatures can fall as low as −94° Fahrenheit (−70° Celsius). However, this bear has adapted to these conditions. Its fur coat is waterproof. It has an excellent sense of smell. It even has slightly webbed toes for swimming between **ice floes** in search of prey. The polar bear's main food source is seals that sit on huge blocks of floating ice. The bear attacks quickly, swatting the seal with its large front paws. The force of the attack kills the seal instantly. Then the bear drags the seal's body somewhere safe where it can eat undisturbed.

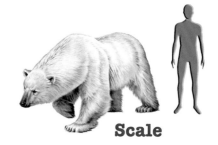

Scale

= Habitat

Where in the World?

The polar bear's scientific name means "marine bear," because it spends many months of the year at sea. Today, polar bears can be found in the Arctic Circle, Canada, Russia, Greenland, on islands off of Norway and Alaska, and on the sea ice that covers the Arctic waters during the winter.

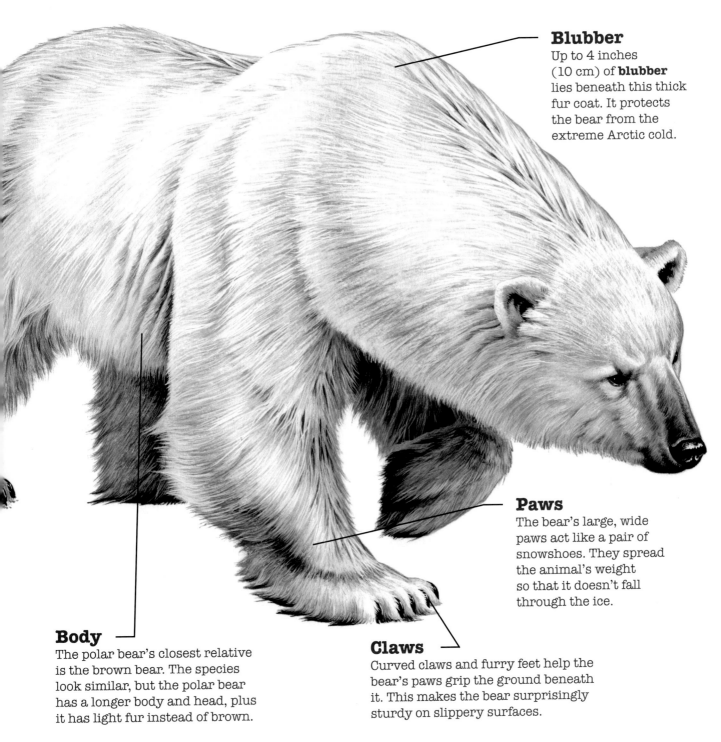

Blubber
Up to 4 inches
(10 cm) of **blubber**
lies beneath this thick
fur coat. It protects
the bear from the
extreme Arctic cold.

Paws
The bear's large, wide
paws act like a pair of
snowshoes. They spread
the animal's weight
so that it doesn't fall
through the ice.

Body
The polar bear's closest relative
is the brown bear. The species
look similar, but the polar bear
has a longer body and head, plus
it has light fur instead of brown.

Claws
Curved claws and furry feet help the
bear's paws grip the ground beneath
it. This makes the bear surprisingly
sturdy on slippery surfaces.

11

A mother polar bear watches over her young cubs.

Ferocious Fact

Polar bears are listed as the first vertebrate animal facing extinction, mostly because of global warming. As sea ice melts earlier each year, the seals that sit on it head to other areas, leaving polar bears little to eat. With climate change worsening, some scientists believe that polar bears could be extinct by 2030.

Every year, it's harder for the bears to find food.

A polar bear sneaks up on an unsuspecting seal.

Polar bears use their sharp teeth to tear through the thick skins of their prey.

Grizzly Bear

Scientific Name: *Ursus arctos horribilis*

The grizzly bear is one of the most feared predators in North America. Its fearsome reputation has resulted in many grizzlies being killed. They are protective of their young and if challenged, they will attack. Grizzlies are expert fishermen. Their favorite fish is salmon. However, since grizzlies are at the top of the forest food chain, they also eat many larger animals, such as moose, elk, and deer. Their powerful paws, claws, and jaws work to bring down these animals with one blow. In some places of the world, humans become the bear's target. Sometimes the only way for a human to survive is to play dead and hope the bear loses interest.

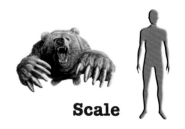

Scale

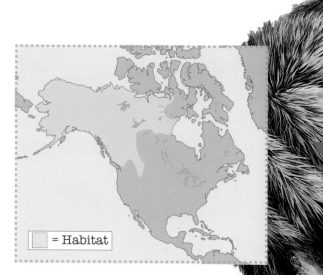

= Habitat

Where in the World?

Grizzly bears once roamed throughout the western United States, Canada, and Mexico. Humans hunting and building on their land has made their numbers decrease. Today, they are mainly found in Alaska, western Canada, and U.S. states near the Rocky Mountains.

Fur
This bear gets its name from its color. Its fur is generally brown, tipped with white. This makes them look **grizzled**.

Back
This distinctive hump covers a mass of muscles attached to the bear's backbone, giving the animal additional strength for digging and catching prey.

Body
The grizzly bear can be distinguished from other bear species by its size, the hump between its shoulders, and its long, curved claws.

Claws
Curved claws on the bear's front feet help with climbing, digging, picking fruit, and catching prey. Claws can be 4 in (10 cm) long.

Ferocious Fact

Grizzly bears are a subspecies of brown bear. These highly adaptable mammals live on grasslands, **scrublands**, and in mountainous, forested regions. Their size depends on the availability of food. Bears that live in areas that have more food tend to be bigger than grizzlies found in places where there is less available to eat.

Grizzly bears have the ability to adapt to all kinds of weather.

Grizzlies have forty-two very sharp teeth.

Did You Know?

- The bear is often thought of as the most famous **hibernator**.

- George Ord gave the grizzly bear its Latin name in 1815. He confused the word "grizzly," meaning streaked with gray, with "grisly," meaning horrible. That is why "horribilis" is in its Latin name.

- These powerful bears can run at speeds of up to 35 mph (56 km/h).

- Grizzly bears have a lifespan of around thirty years in captivity and twenty-five in the wild.

Grizzly bears can stand up to 7 feet (2.1 m) tall.

A man tries to escape a grizzly.

Gray Wolf

Scientific Name: *Canis lupus*

Wolves have been human companions since prehistoric times. Eventually, they evolved into the modern dog. Wolves that stayed away from humans became enemies and were hunted for their fur. The gray wolf still survives today. This adaptable animal will eat almost anything. Smaller prey is killed quickly with a bite to the neck. For bigger animals, wolves work together. First, they use their powerful sense of smell to locate their prey. They then get as close as they can to the animal before attacking. Each wolf takes a different position around the animal and rushes toward their victim, leaping, biting, and clawing until the animal is too tired and weak to fight back.

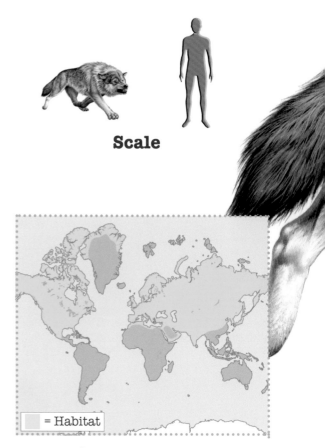

Scale

= Habitat

Where in the World?

At one time the gray wolf was common in all parts of the Northern Hemisphere. Hunting and loss of **habitat** drove the gray wolf out of many places it once lived. Now these animals are found only in areas of northern Asia, Europe, and North America.

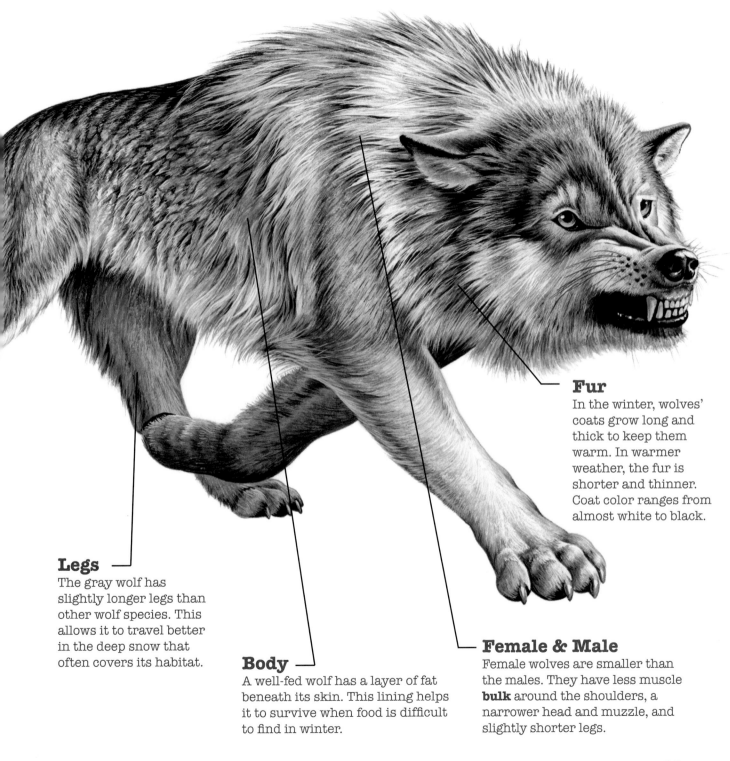

Fur
In the winter, wolves' coats grow long and thick to keep them warm. In warmer weather, the fur is shorter and thinner. Coat color ranges from almost white to black.

Legs
The gray wolf has slightly longer legs than other wolf species. This allows it to travel better in the deep snow that often covers its habitat.

Body
A well-fed wolf has a layer of fat beneath its skin. This lining helps it to survive when food is difficult to find in winter.

Female & Male
Female wolves are smaller than the males. They have less muscle **bulk** around the shoulders, a narrower head and muzzle, and slightly shorter legs.

Baby wolves are called pups.

Wolves howl to call members of their pack together.

Ferocious Fact

When wolf pups are born, they are deaf and blind and have a poor sense of smell. They depend on their senses of taste and touch to move around. For the first few weeks of life, they live inside a den, and are looked after by the mother and other members of the pack.

A wolf pack works together to bring down a moose.

The gray wolf nearly became extinct because of its valuable fur.

Wolverine

Scientific Name: *Gulo gulo*

The wolverine is built like a bear cub, with dagger-like talons and a strong sense of smell that it uses to hunt. Most of the time it preys on small mammals such as mice and rabbits. However, in very cold weather it will attack animals such as moose, which are ten times its own size! The trick is to sneak up on the animal on its snowshoe-like feet and, at the right moment, move closer to its victim in a place where it can't escape. When the animal is trapped, the wolverine sinks its claws into its victim's neck and holds on until the animal dies from blood loss and exhaustion. Powerful jaws mean the wolverine kills its prey quickly.

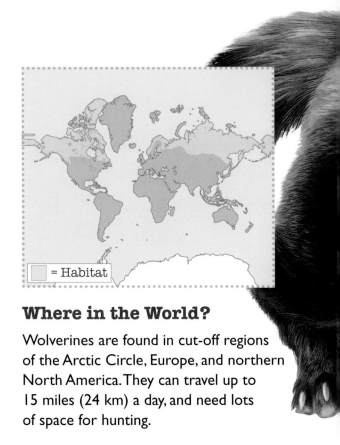

= Habitat

Where in the World?

Wolverines are found in cut-off regions of the Arctic Circle, Europe, and northern North America. They can travel up to 15 miles (24 km) a day, and need lots of space for hunting.

Scale

Scent glands
Wolverines give off a strong-smelling scent, called musk. They use this to mark their territory and help attract a mate.

Jaws
The wolverine's jaws are so strong they can break bones and even eat frozen meat.

Fur
Wolverines have a thick coat of oily brown fur that protects them from the cold. The oil keeps their fur dry.

Legs
A set of short, powerful legs combined with four wide feet help the wolverine to walk easily in the thick snow.

As wolverines travel in their harsh habitat, sometimes they even climb in trees!

Ferocious Fact

The wolverine is not only known for its massive claws and fierce personality, but also for the strong scent it gives off. Like a skunk, the wolverine sprays a bad-smelling liquid, called musk. This has earned it the nicknames of the skunk bear and the stink bear.

A wolverine's paws are formed to cope with thick snow and cold climates.

Did You Know?

- Wolverines belong to the weasel family.

- The wolverine has thirty-eight very sharp teeth.

- European settlers called the wolverine "the **glutton**" because of the huge amount of food it is able to eat in one sitting.

- Newborn wolverines are known as kits.

A wolverine can use its strong jaws to attack a moose and chew through tough materials.

Wolverines are related to weasels, badgers, and ferrets.

Western Diamondback Rattlesnake

Scientific Name: *Crotalus atrox*

The Western diamondback rattlesnake is a pit viper. It uses its rattle on the tip of its tail to warn attackers to stay away. If they don't, it will bite. Sensitive pit organs, or holes behind its nostrils, sense body heat. Usually, it corners its victims. Once it is close enough to strike, long, retractable fangs spring forward. The fangs are hollow, allowing poison to be injected directly into the prey's body. This venom destroys tissue, causes internal bleeding, and ultimately leads to death. Even if the prey manages to get away before the poison takes effect, it will be lucky to escape its ultimate fate in the rattlesnake's belly!

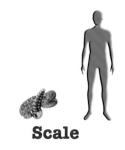

Scale

= Habitat

Where in the World?

Diamondbacks are found from California to the Gulf of Mexico. They prefer dry regions, but inhabit any area where there is a lot for them to eat. They are a ground-dwelling species and particularly prey on reptiles and burrowing mammals.

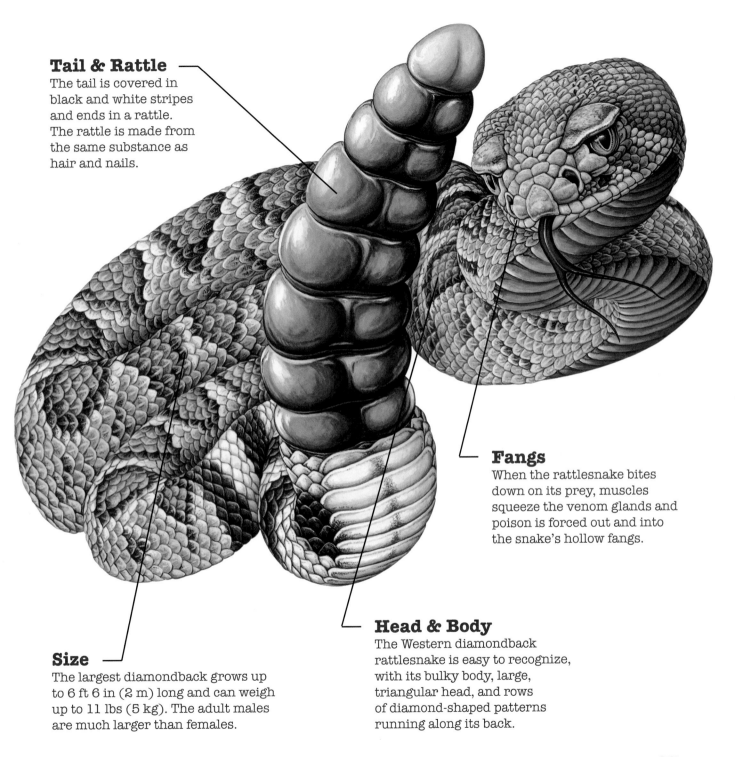

Tail & Rattle

The tail is covered in black and white stripes and ends in a rattle. The rattle is made from the same substance as hair and nails.

Fangs

When the rattlesnake bites down on its prey, muscles squeeze the venom glands and poison is forced out and into the snake's hollow fangs.

Size

The largest diamondback grows up to 6 ft 6 in (2 m) long and can weigh up to 11 lbs (5 kg). The adult males are much larger than females.

Head & Body

The Western diamondback rattlesnake is easy to recognize, with its bulky body, large, triangular head, and rows of diamond-shaped patterns running along its back.

The Western diamondback rattlesnake blends into its desert surroundings.

Ferocious Fact

Every year, an average of fifteen people in the United States die from snake bites. The United States has twenty poisonous snake species found throughout the country, mostly in dry areas like the South or Southwest. The Western diamondback and its eastern relative are the species responsible for most of the deaths, though other snakes bite more people.

Using its fangs, it injects poison into any animals—or people—who may get in its way.

Sensing danger, the snake rattles its tail and raises its head to warn away attackers.

Did You Know?

- Western diamondbacks live up to thirty years in captivity, and up to twenty in the wild.

- A rattlesnake can shake its rattle over sixty times a second for up to three hours at a time!

- Every time the Western diamondback rattlesnake sheds its skin, a new segment of its rattle grows.

- Snakes do not have moveable eyelids. Their eyes are protected by a clear layer that limits eye movement.

A curious coyote ends up hurt after threatening this diamondback.

Glossary

blubber Excessive fat on the bodies of polar bears, whales, and other animals.

bulk The large size of someone or something.

carnivore An animal that eats meat.

glutton A person or animal that eats too much.

grizzled Sprinkled or streaked with gray.

habitat The place or type of place where a plant or animal naturally or normally lives or grows.

hibernator An animal that spends the winter sleeping or resting.

ice floes Large, flat areas of ice floating in the ocean.

nocturnal Active mainly during the night.

pellet A small, hard ball of food.

subspecies A group of related animals; a division of a species.

scrublands Land that is covered with small bushes and trees.

Find Out More

Do you want to learn more about your favorite animals from this book? Check out these books and websites:

Books

Hughes, Catherine D. *National Geographic: Little Kids First Big Book of Animals.* Washington, DC: National Geographic, 2010.

Kolpin, Molly. *Polar Bears.* Mankato, MN: First Facts, 2011.

Spelman, Lucy. *National Geographic Animal Encyclopedia.* Washington, DC: National Geographic, 2012.

Thompson, Bill, III. *The Young Birder's Guide to Birds of Eastern North America.* New York, NY: Houghton Mifflin Harcourt, 2008.

Websites

Meet the Wolverine

www.discovery.com/tv-shows/north-america/animals/wolverine.htm

This short article gives more information about the wolverine.

Kids' Planet ESPECIES Animal Facts Sheets

www.kidsplanet.org/factsheets/map.html

This website lists different animals by region and provides more information about each animal.

Index

barn owl,
    and flying, 6
    habitat preferences, 6
    physical characteristics, 6–9
    predator habits, 6–9

carnivore, 10

gray wolf,
    as pack animals, 18, 20, 21
    habitat preferences, 18, 20
    physical characteristics, 19, 21
    predator habits, 18, 21

grizzly bear,
    habitat preferences, 14, 16
    name origin, 17
    physical characteristics, 14–17
    predator habits, 14, 17

hibernation, 17

nocturnal, 6, 8

polar bear,
    and global warming, 12
    habitat preferences, 10, 12
    physical characteristics, 10–11, 13
    predator habits, 10, 12–13

rattlesnake, Western diamond
    and people, 28
    habitat preferences, 26
    physical characteristics, 26–29
    predator habits, 26, 28–29

wolverine,
    habitat preferences, 22
    musk, 23, 24
    physical characteristics, 22–25
    predator habits, 22, 25